Helping Your Child Live With a Developmental Delay

(A Practical Guide to the Dos and Don'ts)

By Robin L. Atkinson, M.S.

NEW FORUMS

NEW FORUMS PRESS INC.

Published in the United States of America
by New Forums Press, Inc.1018 S. Lewis St.
Stillwater, OK 74074
www.newforums.com

Library of Congress Cataloging-in-Publication Data
Pending

This book may be ordered in bulk quantities at dis-
count from New Forums Press, Inc., P.O. Box 876, Stillwater, OK 74076 [Federal I.D. No. 73 1123239]. Printed
in the United States of America.

ISBN 10: 1-58107-248-1
ISBN 13: 978-1-581072-48-8

Contents

Book Dedication

Undeniably I dedicate this book to God, for without his guidance along every step of this incredible adventure none of these pages would have been written.

Acknowledgements

There are many people who I need to thank for always believing in me and my mission:

To my son Walker: You are my rock!   All I have to do is look at what an amazing young man you are and I know that everything is and always will be all right.

To Keliah, Philip and Rosie: I am so proud of the adults that you have become and the bond that we share.

To my parents: Thank you for instilling in me the independence to always follow my heart, even when it didn't always follow your plan for me. It took a while, but everything worked out just fine. I love you both very much.

To my brothers Rick and Randy: I cherished you when I was five and continue to do so decades later.

To Kim Beair: Without your guidance this project would still be sitting on the shelf. You always seemed to know when I needed a little push to keep me going and your editing expertise made "my voice" even better!

To New Forums Press: Thank You for taking this leap of faith with me. Let's hope that this is just the beginning!

Foreword

Nothing in the world affects us more than concerns for our children and their wellbeing. So imagine, if you will, you have been told that your child has "a developmental delay" "has a disability" "has a genetic syndrome which will affect his/her development" "diagnosis as yet unknown, prognosis undetermined". What a daunting situation...so many questions, so much uncertainty. What do you do? Where do you turn?

As a teacher of early childhood special education for more than thirty years, I understand the questions parents have, and the struggles they are experiencing as they begin their journey so when I approached retirement I worried that there would not be someone to take my place who had the dedication and understanding of families to assume the job of the Early Childhood Special Education Teacher for my school district.

How lucky for all of us that Stillwater Public Schools hired Robin Atkinson!

Robin and I met six years ago and there was an instant connection and friendship. She is passionate about teaching, compassionate toward her students, and most of all an advocate for families. Robin Atkinson has been a teacher for twenty-five years having had experience at every level from twelfth grade to three year olds. Her teaching credentials include co-teaching in the high school regular education classroom to instruction in a self-contained three year old developmentally delayed setting. Her commitment to children extends beyond the classroom through her work with Oklahoma Special Olympics State Games, she is currently the coach for the "Stars of the Future" in Stillwater, and has volunteered her time at her church working with the children there as well. She has been a mentor teacher, special education director, and an active member of the National Education Association, Oklahoma Education Association, and Oklahoma Early Childhood Teachers Association.

Gradually with each teaching experiences Robin became aware that the key to success for developmentally delayed children begins in the early childhood education and identification. Every child and their journey is unique, each of them deserve the best journey that can be. Robin is so committed to making this happen that she envisioned this book! As she began drafting the book, Robin became convinced that this was her "mission" *to empower parents and provide them with a road map to the best possible educational experience for their child.*

Robin Atkinson, in her book *Helping Your Child Live with a Developmental Delay (A Practical Guide to the Do's and Don'ts)* provides answers to the basic questions "Where do I begin?" "What do I do?" "Where is there help?" "How will this affect my family?" "How can I be a positive advocate for my child?" With Robin's help you can determine the best services, strategies and educational experience your child needs. You will learn how to be an advocate for your child and an effective member of your child's educational team. The resources and materials that are provided within this book will help you help your child deal with the daily stressors of peer and adult interactions along with coping, contributing and living within their community. You will be enriched by this material and discover the importance of being an effective communicator and advocate for your child.

Please take advantage of the many resources that Robin provides you for networking with other families. One of the greatest insights you will gain in this book is "You are not alone in this journey."

So, sit back, pen in hand and let Robin assist you as you begin the quest of "Early Childhood Education". It will be unforgettable and full of rewarding results. You will grow as an individual and as a family and your child will be rewarded with a positive educational experience largely because of your advocacy for them.

It is my great honor to recommend *Helping Your Child Live with a Developmental Delay!*

Sincerely,

Jane Turner M.S.
Retired Early Childhood
Special Education Teacher

"How Can I Help You?"

Have you ever had the feeling you were being called to do something? Run a marathon, raise money for a cause, or perhaps write a book? Well that is exactly what happened to me. I have been a special education teacher for 25 years and I know without a doubt it is what I was put on this earth to do. Just recently, however, I realized that I need to be doing more with the knowledge and experience I have gained from my amazing kids and their families.

It is always *so* emotional to sit in a meeting with parents as they are told for the first time that their precious child has a developmental delay. It is intimidating enough for them to sit in a room with professional educators who are discussing their child's development. To then hear the actual words "developmentally delayed" attached to *their own child* during the same meeting can be devastating.

Every parent wants the best for their child and to hear *those* words opens a flood gate of emotions: disbelief, denial, guilt, anger, helplessness. Though it sounds crazy, sometimes those words can also bring a sense relief to *fi-*

nally have some answers. Whatever the feeling might be, the vast majority of parents report the rest of the meeting is a blur and they don't hear another word spoken. I know this look of trauma all too well, and have often wished that I had something to give them that would help make this difficult time easier to comprehend.

After doing some research myself, I became extremely frustrated at the difficulty in finding basic information regarding children with developmental delays in one place. It was then that I realized what I was being called to do: **WRITE THIS BOOK!** Each "chapter" deals with different aspects of raising a child with developmental delays. I know how busy life can be so the chapters are no more than 5 to 7 pages in length. I want you to get the information *you* need in a nonthreatening, reader friendly format; *quick and accurate.* Hopefully this will be your "go to" guide when you have a question and need a quick answer.

As you read this book I want you to feel like you are talking with a friend who knows what you are going through including the raw emotions you feel. I want you to realize you are not alone in this journey. Parents often describe their child's behaviors, and as I nod my head acknowledging I know *exactly* what they are talking about, I repeatedly hear "I thought I was the only one who ever experienced this." I don't want you to feel that way. I want this book to give you some peace of mind that you *can* and *will* face the challenges set before you, while doing what is necessary to help your child become an independent, productive individual. It is my hope that this book can in some small way help you accomplish that goal.

This book is designed to be used in several different ways. You can choose to read it cover to cover in sequential order, or you might want to jump around and read the chapters that seem the most interesting or relevant to you at the time - it really doesn't matter. Each chapter can be read independently if you are just looking for an answer to a question or concern - a quick reference if you will. It can also be read in its entirety in numerical order.

I wanted this book to be something that was inviting to the reader, yet informative at the same time. I know if I see a book that is 3 inches thick I am not likely to read it no matter how interested I am in the topic. I don't have the opportunity to devote the many evenings of uninterrupted quiet time it would take to read something that long with this type of content. By the time I finished I would have to start over because I would have forgotten what I read in the beginning. I know if I don't have time for that, you probably don't either. And by the way, does anyone out there have an abundance of uninterrupted quiet time these days?

My intent for this book is to provide useful tools to help you navigate this journey of awareness, discovery, and enlightenment. Awareness of the developmental delay with which your child lives, discovery of how empowered your child will become, and enlightenment as you see what your child will accomplish with your help and encouragement.

I am honored that you have chosen to read my book. It truly was a labor of love and I wanted it to express the joy I receive from working with children and their families who live with developmental delays. It is because of them that this book was written. To all my past, present and future students and their families I say "THANK YOU" for giving me the courage, inspiration and drive to write this book!

Developmental Delay... What's That?

"Your present circumstances don't determine where you go: they merely determine where you start."

— Nido Oubein

Hearing the words developmental delay for the first time with regard to your child can be extremely scary and confusing. Depending on the state in which you live, it can also have differing definitions. I hope I can put you at ease by giving you a basic understanding of the term "developmental delay." In my current school district, DD basically means that a child who exhibits a 50% delay in their developmental age compared to their chronological age (how old they really are) is considered to have a developmental delay. This can occur in several different ways. There are five (5) areas that are looked at when considering whether or not a delay is present: (1) cognitive, (2) physical, (3) communication, (4) social and emotional, and (5) adaptive. We will talk more about what each one of these means a bit later, but for now let's just think about it this way, if a child is 2 years old, but is only functioning at the communication level of a 1 year old, then he would be considered to have a 50% delay in communication. If a child is only exhibiting behaviors of a child half his age he would be considered developmentally delayed.

Now let's muddy the water a little further. In some states, including my own, if a child presents with a 25% delay in two areas of development such as cognitive and communication, then he would also be considered to be living with developmental delays. This formula is not universal but something similar is in place in each school district around the country. You simply need to go to the Board of Education website in your particular state to see their criteria.

There is one other way to determine eligibility for a developmental delay. If there has been a diagnosed physical or mental condition that has a high probability of resulting in a delay. Some of those diagnoses are: chromosomal disorders, genetic disorders, neurological abnormalities, or identified syndromes. This is not a complete list by any means, but just a sampling of what might be considered as a diagnosed developmental delay. It musts be noted that just because there is a diagnosed developmental delay **Does Not** mean that the child will qualify for educational services.

There will still need to be a 50% delay in one or a 25% delay in at least two of the evaluated domains to be considered for special education.

I mentioned earlier about the five (5) areas that are evaluated when considering whether or not a child lives with a developmental delay. These five areas are the standard criteria across the nation. Let's take some time and look at each one of these areas individually and discuss what they are and why they are important for a child's development.

Let's look at Cognitive skills first. Basically, this is what you might refer to as the child's intellectual ability. In very young children, things like recognizing their name when called or differentiating between two objects are examples of this skill. These are the initial stages of being able to retain and retrieve information. It has to do with short and long term memory and the ability to comprehend new information. These skills are the building blocks for all learning for the rest of your child's life. When evaluating infants and very young children, most of the evaluation tools are questionnaires that the parent either fills out or answers orally. After around age two there are some standardized tests requiring the child to perform tasks that can be accomplished by children in the same basic age group. Usually the assessment is a combination of parent check lists and child performance tests that will determine if a child has a developmental delay in the area of cognition.

The next skill we will look at is communication. If you are like most people, the word communication is used to describe the ability to speak - but communication is much more than that. For the purpose of evaluating for a speech and/or language impairment there are two areas of concern; **Speech** and **Language**.

Speech includes (1) oral-motor skills, (2) articulation, and (3) fluency. For young children the concentration in my opinion should be on oral-motor skills. This starts from the very beginning with a baby sucking on a bottle, graduating to a sippy cup and then beginning to chew soft foods. All these things play a very important role in the development of language. What I would consider the next area of importance is voice and the ability to control its volume. If you have spent any time around young children you will know what I am talking about. They are either so soft spoken that you can't hear a word they are saying or they are so loud that your head is pounding like you've just been to a hard rock concert. I think I might have just shown my age there, anyway, moving on. Articulation and fluency are developmental skills and usually will come along for the ride once the mouth and voice have figured out what they are supposed to do.

The second area of concern is "Language" and this involves *receptive ability* (what is being heard or taken in auditorally) and *expressive ability* (what is being spoken or produced verbally). When dealing with very young children these two areas are usually looked at the most. There is a direct correlation to a child's language skills and his cognitive ability. It makes sense if you think about it. If a child knows the information but can't express it, then it appears as if he doesn't know it in the first place. Many times after a child has worked with a speech and language pathologist and improved these language skills, the child's cognitive scores go up as well.

Physical or motor skills are broken into two separate areas. *Fine motor skills* are the ability to use your hands and fingers. Holding a crayon, using pinchers or tongs, and stringing beads are all considered to be fine motor skills, there are many more, but you get the idea. This skill is important for obvious reasons, if you can't use your hands and fingers appropriately there will be some difficult times ahead for you. *Gross motor skills* are the second area in this domain. Some of the skills evaluated are walking, jumping, hopping, and skipping. Many children who are diagnosed with muscular disabilities will have problems in this specific skill set. Many children who have no apparent physical issues can still have trouble with gross motor skills. Environmental factors can sometimes be the cause of this and it can be a reason for concern that might not have surfaced without the initial evaluation. Once again, early intervention is key.

The fourth area we will discuss is the social and emotional ability of a child. A simple way to define this is by asking "how does your child interact with peers and adults?" Learning how to share, taking turns, and acknowledging the other people in the same space with you are very necessary skills. In many cases I have parents tell me their child doesn't interact at all, and depending on the age of the child that can explain a lot about the their social makeup. The second question is "does your child seem to become overly emotional for little or no reason?" Now don't get me wrong, the 2 year olds occasional temper tantrum in the middle of the grocery store does not constitute an emotional delay. If, however, that 2 year old has a tantrum every time your family goes out in public, then it would be reason for concern. Humans are a social and emotional species and being able to interact and respond appropriately in different public and private settings are very important skills to acquire.

The last skill set we will look at is adaptive. For the most part this involves self-help and transitioning skills. Depending on the age of your child, things like potty training, dressing independently, and eating are considered when looking at self-help skills. Obviously these are skills that you need for daily living. A few of the things looked at in the area of transitions is how easily your child separates from you, moves from one activity or physical space to another, and complies with home/school rules. This is by no means a comprehensive list of all the things that are considered when assessing adaptive skills, but it does give you a good idea of what the term means.

Please remember that just because your child may present with developmental delays right now, it does not mean they will always have them. In many cases early intervention will help eliminate the problems before they become permanent issues in your child's life. I know that this is not the case for many of you reading this book, and you already know that your child's developmental issue is going to be a life long journey. For you, I applaud the fact that you are being proactive and taking an active role in creating a positive outlook for your child's future. Children emulate what they see their parents doing, and if they see you working hard on their behalf they will work hard for themselves as well. So to you I say "job well done!"

All Those Acronyms!

"Believe you can and you are half way there."
— Theodore Roosevelt

One thing is certain; when it comes to abbreviations, text messaging has nothing on the world of Special Education. It has a language all its own, and for a new comer it can be very confusing. We don't mean to speak in code; it's just quicker to use the acronyms, as you can see in the list below. If you are in a meeting and the test evaluator, special education teacher, and related service providers all start using a lot of abbreviations that you don't understand do not hesitate to stop them and ask what each one means. You can't be an integral part of the team if you do not comprehend what is being said in the meeting. Sometimes those of us who have been in the field for a very long time forget that not everyone knows what a MEEGS is. Don't worry by the time you finish reading this chapter you will and several other acronyms that are most commonly used. Many of these will vary by a letter or two, depending on where you live, but I think that most will be relatively close and you should be able to figure them out. If you can't ask! There is no shame in wanting to become more knowledgeable especially when it concerns your child.

I know this list is lengthy, but you will be glad you have it at some point when you need a quick reference.

AAIDD – American Association of Intellectual and Developmental Disabilities
ADA – American with Disabilities Act
ADD – Attention Deficit Disorder
ADHD – Attention Deficit Hyperactivity Disorder
APE – Adaptive Physical Education
APR – Annual Performance Report
ARNP – Advanced Registered Nurse Practitioner
ASD – Autism Spectrum Disorders
ASHA – American Speech Language Hearing Association
AT – Assistive Technology
BIP – Behavior Intervention Plan
CARG-A – Curriculum Access Resource Guide-Alternate
CARG-M – Curriculum Access Resource Guide-Modified
CEC – Council for Exceptional Children
CHADD – Children and Adults with Attention Deficit Hyperactivity Disorder
CRT – Criterion-Referenced Test
DD – Developmental Delay
DDSD – Developmental Disabilities Service Division

DHS — Department of Human Services
DSM — Diagnostic and Statistical Manual
ECCO — Enriching Children's Communication Opportunities
ED — Emotional Disabilities
EI — Early Intervention
EIS — Early Intervening Services
ELL — English Language Learner
EPSDT — Early Periodic Screening Diagnosis and Treatment
ESA — Educational Service Agency
ESEA — Elementary and Secondary Education Act
ESY — Extended School Year
FAPE — Free Appropriate Public Education
FBA — Functional Behavioral Assessment
FEOG — Full Educational Rights and Privacy Goal
FERPA — Family Educational Rights and Privacy Act
FM — Focused Monitoring
GED — General Educational Development
HI — Hearing Impairment
ID — Intellectual Disabilities
IEE — Independent Educational Evaluation
IEP — Individual Educational Plan
IFSP — Individualized Family Service Plan
IDEA — Individuals with Disabilities Education Act
IHE — Institution of Higher Education
IQ — Intelligence Quotient
LD — Learning Disabilities

LEA — Local Educational Agency
LEP — Limited English Proficient
LRE — Least Restrictive Environment
MAAP — Modified Alternate Assessment Program
MEEGS — Multidisciplinary Evaluation and Eligibility Group Summary
MOE — Maintenance of Effort
NAEP — National Assessment of Educational Progress
NASDSE — National Assessment of State Directors of Special Education
NCLB — No Child Left Behind Act
NIMAS — National Instructional Materials Accessibility Standard
O & M — Orientation and Mobility
OCR — Office of Civil Rights
OHI — Other Health Impairment
OI — Orthopedic Impairment
OJA — Office of Juvenile Affair
OSEP — Office of Special Education Programs
OT — Occupational Therapy
PBIS — Positive Behavioral Interventions and Supports
PE — Physical Education
PGARD — Professional Group on Attention Deficits and Related Disorders
PL 94-142 — Public Law 94-142
PT — Physical Therapy
PTI — Parent Training and Information Center
RED — Review of Existing Data
RtI — Response to Intervention

SBE — State Board of Education
SLP — Speech Language Pathologist
SOP — Summary of Performance
SLD — Specific Learning Disabilities
SSA — Social Security Administration
TBI — Traumatic Brain Injury
USDE — United States Department of Education
VI — Visual Impairment

Well there you go; I told you it was long. Please don't get overwhelmed by it. By no means will you encounter the entire list at the same time, but you will probably see many of these acronyms through the course of your child's life. I will also be using these acronyms throughout the rest of this book, so you may need to refer back to these pages if necessary. Reading them within the book will also help you to become familiar with them and how they are used within the context of special education.

Routines and Transitions

"Don't prepare the path for the child; prepare the child for the path."
— Anonymous

When you think about your morning routine what comes to mind? For me its bathroom, coffee, shower, dress, makeup, hair...you get the idea. Most of us have a routine that we follow and we don't even realize it. If for some reason it gets interrupted or changed it can throw off the whole day. How about when you are in the middle of something? Let's say you are watching your favorite TV show and your doorbell rings. You go answer it and miss the last 10 minutes of your show. There was no closure for you and you have to wait for the next episode to see what happened – it's frustrating! It is the same thing that happens when your child has a change in routine or is asked to move from one activity to another before he/she is ready. As adults we have learned to cope with these situations, but for children (especially those living with a developmental delay) this can cause a complete meltdown with crying, screaming, kicking, and even head banging (and not the musical kind). This seems extreme and concerning for parents and it can be tempting to avoid changes to your child's routine at all costs. It may seem a whole lot easier to just wait for your child to be "ready" before attempting to move on to a new activity.

Please don't do that! It is not real life; change happens and interruptions will occur. The sooner your child learns to cope with it the easier life will be for everyone involved. Don't get me wrong, when you do make a change *be ready.* I have literally had everything in my classroom swiped off the tables and onto the floor. It is not a pretty sight, however, for many children this is the only way they know how to communicate to me what they are feeling. When this happens at your home please remember, this is not a time to punish, but it is a time to wait your child out, a battle of the wills so to speak. You MUST NOT give in. It can take a while the first several times. During these outbursts is a time when the saying "less is more" comes into play. Your child only will hear the first few words that come out of your mouth and the rest will sound like Charlie Brown's teacher: Wah,wah, wah, wah. The key phrases that I suggest you use are "I will wait" "When you're ready" and "I will help you". Then do exactly that - wait until they are finished throwing the tantrum, be ready to give them what they need (hug, high five, I love you) and help them move on. This is the perfect time to teach them different ways to let you know what they are feeling. Begin using sign language for simple words or phrases: "I am mad, sad, or scared", "I am sorry", "Help please". Many times children just need to remove themselves from the situation for a few minutes. I strongly suggest that you have a special place in your home that your child can go where he/she feels safe and can regroup. This does not get them out of completing the task they were asked to do, it just gives them a few minutes to pull themselves together.

I encourage you to keep an informal log on the length of each outburst. It may feel like things aren't getting any better, but if you keep a log I promise you will see a decrease in the amount of time and intensity of each episode until they will finally be eliminated altogether. The other thing to remember during this time is if a mess was made or the area needs to be cleaned up that will still need to happen. It is fine to let them know you will help them clean up, but by no means should you let them off the hook and do it all for them. The only thing that reinforces is "If I throw a fit I won't have to do what was asked of me in the first place". Mark my words you will be tested. Children want to know if you really mean what you say and if you mean it every single time. Once they figure out that you do mean it the struggles will stop and one day you will look up and your child will be picking up his/her toys before you have even asked them to. I know some of you are rolling your eyes right now and saying "Yeah right, you never met my kid" and your right I haven't, but I've met hundreds of other kids and this method works. Believe it or not kids want to know what is expected of them and once they realize what that is they are very willing to play by the rules.

Some other strategies that have proven very successful when working with small children are picture schedules, a first this then that card, small rewards, and a timer. As I mentioned earlier children are just like us when it comes to unexpected change - they don't like it. A picture schedule can be very effective to let a child know what his/her day will consist of. I have found that they work best when I have actual photographs of the child doing the activities which will go on the picture schedule for that day. For example one might look like this for a morning routine: breakfast, brush teeth, get dressed, TV time. Each one of those activities would have an actual photograph of the child doing it. You can use a small photo book to put them in so it is portable. For a very easy way to make one that will stay at home, get a piece of poster board 4 to 6 inches wide, put a strip of Velcro down the center, put smaller pieces of the opposing side of the Velcro on the pictures, then just put them in the order that they will occur for that day. It doesn't matter if it goes vertical or horizontal. You might want to put a "finished" box at the end of the schedule so that after each activity is completed the child can pull it off and put it in the box. Make sure to ALWAYS include a desired activity within the schedule. Children want to know there is something worth working for and for young children 3 to 4 things on the schedule at a time is plenty. After those are finished put up the next 3 or 4 tasks.

Sometimes children need things even more simplified so a First this, Then that card works great. Again you will want pictures of the child doing the different activities. The first picture (First this) will be of something that you need the child to do or it is something that you know the child does not particularly like to do. The next picture (Then that) will be of something the child desires: play with trains, a special toy, or a piece of popcorn. I also use this method when I am getting children to try new food. Pictures are not needed because you have the food right there. Just say "first apple then yogurt" or whatever two foods you are working with. In the beginning, even if the child touches the apple to their lips or licks it consider that a victory and let them have the yogurt. Please remember small victories are victories all the same.

I touched on small rewards a little bit and I use them all the time, however not everyone is a fan of them because they don't think children should be "bribed" to do something.

My philosophy is that if I can get a child to be successful at whatever we are trying to accomplish then they deserve a reward. Now please hear me on this, I am not talking about a whole bag of fish crackers or the entire length of the Thomas the Train video. I am saying one fish cracker or 5 minutes of the video. These can even be replaced with high fives and hugs after the desired behavior or skill is becoming more consistent and then all reinforcement can be eliminated after mastery has been achieved.

One last strategy that works really well is the use of a timer. Kitchen timers work great, they make a quiet ticking sound so your child can hear that it is working and it rotates so the time can be seen ticking away. One of the ways I use my timer is when we are working on the skill of staying on task. I usually start with only 30 seconds to one minute and increase the time every day or week depending on how well the child is doing. The other great way to use a timer is to set it for 5 minutes, two minutes, whatever you choose and warn your child, "I am setting the timer for 5 minutes, when it goes off it will be time to….". I usually let them know when it is at 2 minutes as well just to help them remember that it is almost time to move to something else. The great thing about using a timer is that it takes the blame off of you, the timer is telling your child how long they need to work on the activity or when it is time to stop whatever they are doing and move to the next thing.

You will need to try some of these different approaches to see which ones will work best for you and your child. Many of them work well together such as the picture schedule and the timer. There is no right or wrong way to incorporate them into your daily life so just experiment and see what is the best fit for your family's situation. It is my hope that at least some of these suggestions will help to bring some harmony into the everyday life of raising your child.

The last piece to this puzzle is the supporting cast. Everyone that has regular interaction with your child must also know what the rules are and abide by them. That means grandparents and other family members, daycare workers, related service providers, teachers, etc. Everyone needs to be on the same page when it comes to teaching your child appropriate ways to handle difficult situations. Typically developing children are expected to behave appropriately in all different types of settings and you should not expect any less from your child. It may take a little longer to get there, but it will happen as long as you are clear and consistent with your expectations. Nobody said it would be easy, but if you do it now while your child is very young, you will reap the benefits for years to come.

Finding the Perfect Fit

"Inclusive, good quality education is a foundation for dynamic and equitable societies."
— Desmond Tutu

For many families, deciding what will be appropriate for them and their child is an exhausting task. There are so many different programs, therapies, specialists, and theories available these days that it's literally a smorgasbord of choices. What works for one family does not necessarily work for, or is not appropriate for another family. Please be careful when someone says to you, "This program works for ALL children". No program works for ALL children. It has been my experience that a combination of different programs is usually the most effective approach for each individual child. You want your child to be a well-rounded person, experiencing all kinds of different things. It may take some experimenting with several programs to see what combination your child will respond to.

As I mentioned in a previous chapter, speech and language as well as motor skills are two areas that are evaluated when determining if there is a developmental delay of some kind. If these areas are found to be of concern, it is likely a program with speech and language therapy, occupational therapy, and physical therapy will be recommended for your child. Music therapy is another wonderful intervention that I have found to be extremely beneficial for children living with developmental delays. You are probably thinking "wow, how in the world do we decide what to try?" This is where your physician, early intervention specialist, your state's specified DD program, your county health department, and local public school special education departments can help. You can give any of these agencies a phone call and they can guide you in the right direction. What follows is just a brief explanation of what each of the different programs that I mentioned earlier can offer you and your child.

For many parents the first sign that there might be developmental issues is when verbal language seems to be absent or lacking. This can happen for several reasons. There is no need to talk; all the child's needs are being met by parents, siblings, grandparents, etc. I'm sure you know exactly what I'm talking about - the child points, whines, or grunts until the adult or siblings figure out what the child is wanting. Need is met, no need for words. Another reason might be just a lack of exposure. It is so very important that you talk to your child, particularly when they are crying or whining for something. Say to them "Oh you want a drink of juice." Then hand them the cup with juice in it, or "Do you want your blanket?" Hold up the blanket. This gives your child a label for the particular object they are wanting.

Processing delays or hearing loss could be more serious reasons your child isn't verbalizing. In both of these cases evaluations and screenings can be done to help determine the cause. Consult your doctor or health care provider and they can refer you to the appropriate agency. In many cases this can be done at your local county health department at no cost to you. After the evaluation is complete, you will be asked to sign a release of information so the results can be sent to either the early intervention agency in your area or your local public school system (ages 3 and up).

I mention language first because in many cases with young children, a language problem may also look like problems in other areas such as cognitive and personal/social skills. When children do not have expressive language to tell you what they want, or receptive language to process what you request, it may appear they have deficits in their intellectual ability. This is also problematic when dealing with social issues. When a child does not have the words to get their point across they sometimes use pushing, pinching, biting, and crying. This is why the social/emotional domain is also affected by language or the lack of it. Once some of the language concerns are addressed in many cases some of the other issues will be eliminated as well. On occasion the language concerns are rectified, but the child still reverts to the old habits of communicating. This is nothing to be worried about. Parents can contact a counselor who understands these issues to learn some quick strategies to nip the bad habits in the bud that have been formed as a result of the DD.

Another area that you will see early in your child's life is the development of his/her motor skills. Gross motor skills such as crawling, standing, and walking are the more obvious things that you will see. These skills involve balance, which in turn also involve hearing or the lack of it. If your child seems off balance or overly clumsy it can be as simple as clogged or infected ears. Once that is cleared up you will see a vast improvement in this area. If that is not the issue a Physical Therapist could be recommended to help you figure out what the problem is. Some of your child's fine motor skills involve grasping, pinching, eating and drinking. There is a natural progression when discussing fine motor skills; it usually goes from a rudimentary hand grasp to a more refined finger grip on utensils, and writing instruments. The strength of the hands is also something that is looked at and if any of these areas are cause for concern you will more than likely be recommended to an Occupational Therapist.

I'm sure that right about now you are thinking, "how in the world am I supposed to coordinate seeing all of these people?" Here's the good news, all of these services: speech/language therapy, physical therapy and occupational therapy can be facilitated through either your county program or through your public school, depending on the age of your child. Take advantage of these programs - that is what they are there for.

The last type of therapy I will discuss is Music Therapy. This is not available in all areas and is usually not a program that will be covered within the state and federal programs. In those lucky areas where it is offered I **strongly** recommend you take advantage of it. Music Therapy is not just listening to music or singing children's songs. There is extensive research to validate the successes of Music Therapy. Locate a Music Therapist in your area if you feel it could help your child. I work in one of the lucky school districts that "get it", and we contract with a certified Music Therapist. I have seen firsthand how it has enabled numerous children to communicate through music when nothing else has worked. Unfortunately this is not the norm across the country and paying for private music therapy sessions can be expensive. The benefit is that many of the therapist's techniques can be adapted by you on a more simplified scale with some direction. Go to your library and check out a book or look it up on the internet. That would be better for your child than no music exposure at all.

There are certainly more services out there than I have mentioned in this chapter, but speech/language, occupational, and physical therapies are the most widely used. These three are the ones that are federally funded and what you will find consistently in the public schools. Music Therapy is my personal favorite because I have seen such dramatic results in the children who have been involved with it.

I have mentioned it before, but it is worth reiterating; starting these therapies early is extremely important. You know your child better than anyone else, and if you feel there might be a problem, do not hesitate to voice those concerns to your physician. It is better to have your concerns evaluated and either be ruled out or validated and addressed appropriately.

Let's All Calm Down

"Courage is fear that said its prayers"
— Dorothy Bernard

For many children who live with a developmental delay, crowded or loud places, certain textures of food, and even being outside if it is windy, cold, or hot can be extremely difficult. This is usually because they are experiencing sensory overload. In most cases just finding something that calms them during these episodes is enough to help them work through the experience and move on. In this chapter we will talk about some calming techniques that have proven helpful.

One of the things that seem to work for many children is deep pressure massage or squeezes as we call them. Have you ever had a massage or just had your neck and shoulders rubbed? Think about how much more relaxed and calm you were after that. It works the same way for children. Just stand behind them and give their head or shoulders a consistent squeeze or use a paint roller and go up and down the arms and legs - this will allow your child to relax. Weighted vests and blankets can be used as well. Once children realize how much these things help them they will come to you and ask for them. I even have students in the middle of a meltdown come to me and say "hug me", "squeeze", or "vest on" because they know it feels good and it allows them to release the tension that has built up in their body. Things that vibrate can also be very beneficial: pillows, back massagers, and vibrating chair liners work great. Introduce the object to your child by showing them what it does and then allow them to hold it or place their hand on it then just sit back and watch what they will do. Many children will sit on the pillow or lay their head on it. With the hand held back massager children might hold it on the top or back of their head. In my experience it is usually immediate as to whether I child finds vibration comforting or not. Please keep in mind this will not work for all children. If your child resists this strategy after trying it a few times discontinue doing it. You can try again at a later date, but for those children who don't like to be touched at all, deep pressure and vibration are probably not good techniques to use. Don't get discouraged, there are several other things you can try. You and your child will figure out what works best.

The second thing that many children find very calming is swinging. The motion of it helps get the body centered. Hammocks are wonderful for this for several reasons. You can put them inside or outside and most of them are easy to put up and take down. This is something that you can do with your child. Climb in the hammock and go for a gentle swing. You will both end up feeling more relaxed. If you don't have a hammock get a sheet or blanket and you can swing your child in that. This will take two people or you will need to securely tie one end of the sheet or blanket to something sturdy.

For those children who need to block out some of the extraneous noise get some headphones. The ones that cover the entire ear work best, they will knock out the most sound. Make sure you cut off the cord so they won't trip or get it wrapped around their neck. They will be right in style since all the big athletes and young music celebrities are all wearing them as well.

Music is also a wonderful way for children to calm down. Make sure that if your child is upset and needing to decompress, pick music that is slow and rhythmic. Studies show that music with fewer beats per minute will help slow down the heart rate and regulate the breathing of a person. Singing familiar songs is another great way to bring your child back to a more positive frame of mind. Music and singing are just natural ways to make you feel better. Think about it. When you see a person walking around humming a song you don't have to ask them how they are feeling. You already know they are in a good mood and feeling fine, so use music to help keep an upbeat atmosphere in your home.

There are times when it is ok for your child to escape to their "happy" place. That does not always mean physically leaving the area. When you see that they are starting to become flustered it is ok to allow your child to do whatever it is that comforts them for a few minutes, some self-stimulation that makes them feel better (rocking, hand flapping, saying the ABC's, etc). Once they have calmed themselves down they will be able to continue the task at hand.

Every child is different and will have their own special thing that makes them feel safe and calm. Just be observant to what your child repeatedly does to instinctively comfort themselves. That will let you know what to do or offer to them when the need arises. There is one last thing I strongly encourage you to do. When you know you and your child will be going into a situation or doing something that will be difficult for your child, let them know well in advance that it is coming. Talk about what is going to happen; practice how to interact with others, role play different situations that your child might find himself in, and always reassure your child that everything will be all right. Your child will follow your lead. If you are uptight and nervous about a situation then your child will sense that and be apprehensive as well. If they see you dealing with situations in a calm, controlled manner they are more apt to stay calm themselves. Don't get me wrong, there will be meltdowns - but if you are in the right frame of mind, you will be able to deal with it better and your child will too.

The Family Dynamic

Life is a song – sing it
Life is a game- play it
Life is a challenge – meet it
Life is a dream – realize it
Life is a sacrifice – offer it
Life is love – enjoy it
— Jai Baba

Under the best circumstances, juggling a family's hectic schedule can be demanding. Combine that with the added responsibilities of caring for a child with a developmental delay and life can become overwhelming. Other siblings can feel neglected, spouses have no time for each other, and extended family members have all the answers. All of these people play an important role in the family dynamic and it is imperative that each one knows where and how they fit into this complicated puzzle.

For the "typically" developing children in the family it can become frustrating because so much attention is being given to the child living with a special need. Sometimes behaviors surface in the "typical" children that were previously absent such as hyperactivity, aggressiveness, and sulking to name a few. Oftentimes very young siblings see their brother or sister getting a lot of attention, and due to lack of vocabulary they begin to act out as their only way to communicate frustration. Make sure to carve out time for each of your children. Set aside a special day or event once a month that each child gets "alone time" with each parent - if you can swing it. If you both can't be gone at the same time then alternate each month so that your children realize they are important to both their mother and father. A couple of hours a month can and will go a long way to promote a more harmonious atmosphere in your home.

For those of you who are married, take time to be a couple. I cannot stress this enough. Just as I pointed out about spending time with your children, you must find time to spend with each other. This is a "no children" time zone. Call it what you will: date night, a parent party, or big people time. What you call it doesn't matter as much as making sure you find time as a couple to enjoy time without the kids. Take time to rekindle and remember how important each of you is to the other. If you are not married and many of us aren't, it is equally important that you find time to take care of yourself. It is okay to want to do adult things once in a while. Having a child who lives with a developmental delay doesn't define who you are; it is just a part of your total self. Go out with friends now and then, exercise, take a bubble bath or get up a little early just to sit in a quiet house before the rest of the family wakes up. If you don't take care of yourself you will not be any good to anyone else when they need you. Don't think of "me time" as being selfish, it is anything but that. You must be healthy both physically and mentally so that when it comes time to deal with the stressors of raising your family you will be in the right frame of mind to do so.

For many parents, extended relatives, such as grandparents, aunts, uncles, and cousins play an important role in the care of the children within the family. Their advice and input can be invaluable, and in most cases good intentioned. It can, at times, also be intimidating, intrusive, and sometimes hurtful. When your child is living with a developmental delay and is not reaching all of the milestones both physically and emotionally at the typical rate this can and in many cases does cause conflict within the family unit. Relatives will tell you "If you would just do…. then this would happen" or "If you didn't allow…you wouldn't have this problem". Please remember the term developmental delay means just that. Your child will reach most if not all of those milestones, but at a different rate than the national average of typically developing children. The term doesn't mean that they can't or won't reach them at all. You know your child better than any other person in this world, so as long as you are comfortable with the plan that you, your child's doctors and service providers have created, then go with your instincts. If you are seeing developmental growth, even if it is not as rapid as some might think it should be, then feel confident making decisions on what is appropriate or not for YOUR child. When all is said and done you will be the one still there advocating for your child. Hopefully some of the naysayers will see what a fabulous job you are doing and jump on the bandwagon with you.

Family dynamics and relationships can be a very rocky boat in the best of circumstances so when a child arrives who also has a developmental delay it can cause added stress to the situation. It is very important that everyone in the family knows first that they are loved and valued and second that they know what their role is within the family unit. Many times we as parents assume that our children know that we love them, when in fact they don't. Take the time to show them that you love each of them for their very own uniqueness. Keep your spouse an important part of your life - he or she is your strongest supporter when you feel like you can't handle anymore. If you are single take time for yourself, be an adult with a name, not just "Sissy's mom." Find someone - a friend, a sibling, even another parent to be a sounding board who will just listen when you need to vent. Lastly, let all of the good intentioned relatives know how much you appreciate their love and concern. Make them aware of the plan that has been put into place specifically for your child and encourage them to be a part of that plan if they so desire. You have now let everyone know who is in charge of your child's upbringing (you) and you have given them an option to participate in a way that you are comfortable with. They will either jump on board and become a positive supporter of you and your child or they will bow out gracefully. Either way your child's best interests are being met and you don't have to second guess yourself because of external "advice" from loved ones. Lastly, please remember, family is the core of all relationships and there is no greater bond than those among its members, so keep those you love close to your heart.

Being a Team Player

"Alone we can do so little, together we can do so much."

— Helen Keller

This is the chapter I promised that you would want to have the acronym list handy. When it comes to placing a child into special education there are several components to be considered. This is not because the educational personnel are trying to confuse anyone; in most cases it is because they want what is the best, the most appropriate and the least restrictive learning environment for your child. It is your job to be ready to inform them about his/her strengths and weaknesses, likes and dislikes, eating and sleeping habits, services that they are or have received in private settings, etc. As I have said before, no one knows your child better than you do so the more information you are willing to share the easier it will be to make accurate recommendations for them.

The team, which consists of you the parent, an administrator, the school psychologist, special education teacher and sometimes related service providers such as the speech pathologist and OT/PT must review existing Data (REDS form) to determine what further testing still needs to be done to consider special education placement. At this point a meeting will be scheduled to obtain parent consent for testing and evaluation. Observations and parent interviews will usually to be done at this time as well. All of this information will be interpreted and placed on the MEEGS form. There will then be another meeting to go over these findings and determine if a developmental delay exists. Once the determination has been made the team must decide what the placement will look like. There are several options to consider.

The school district must offer an educational placement that is comparable to what they offer for typically developing children of the same age. For example if the district has a half day Pre-K program for typically developing 4 year olds then they need to have at least the same for their developmentally delayed children of that age in the district. Most school districts do not have programs for their typically developing 3 year old children so when a child who is living with a developmental delay turns 3 the team will need to decide what is going to be the most appropriate placement for them.

I think it is important to mention two things here, one if a school district does not have a general education program for 3 or 4 year olds the only thing they are obligated to provide for the DD family is related services (speech/ language, OT and PT). The second thing to remember is that if the district does have a DD program for 3 year olds you as the parent, have the choice to place them in the public school, to keep them at home, or you may choose to have your child attend a private daycare facility and pay that tuition yourself. If you chose one of the last two options you could bring your child to their home school to receive related services if they qualified for any or all of them. I highly recommend that you do some research and find out exactly what programs are available in your specific school district.

Once the determination has been made that your child does present with a developmental delay an IEP (Individual Educational Program) will be created. This includes all of the services that will be provided, along with annual goals and short term objectives that are specific to your child's needs. The amount of time your child will be receiving related services and direct instruction from the special education teacher will also be documented on the services page. It is imperative that there be an open line of communication between all of the team members and that all voices are heard during this process. If you are uncomfortable, unclear, or want something added/deleted to the IEP please speak up. This is the time to talk things through so that your child receives the most optimum program available. How the services will be provided can occur in a number of ways: full day, half day, 2 or 3 days per week for younger children, or homebound (medically fragile children may be considered for this placement). In my 3 year old DD program the students come 2 half days per week, in either morning or afternoon. So as you can see there is no set way the placement should look. It is what the team decides is the most appropriate and least restrictive for each individual child.

Let me just say right now that I am a huge proponent of inclusion in the regular classroom setting whenever possible. I believe that it is the most beneficial placement for all children involved, developmentally delayed and typically developing children alike. It is a win-win situation when it is done correctly. What the inclusion looks like will differ depending on the severity of the delay; medical issues of the child and to be quite honest the supports that are available within the school setting. Inclusion will not work if the student AND the regular education teacher are not given the appropriate tools to ensure success for everyone involved in the process. Just placing a special needs child in the regular classroom and having them stay over in a corner working only with a paraprofessional is NOT inclusion. The word inclusion comes from the root word to "include". This may also look differently from year to year. In the early years when your child is just beginning school, let's say in Pre-K, the IEP team may decide that socialization is the most important issue to address so total inclusion in the regular Pre-K classroom surrounded by typically developing children to help develop social skills may be what is recommended. However, as the years progress and academics become more of a priority, some direct one on one instruction might become more appropriate for your child. She might need to be pulled out of the regular classroom in order for that to happen. Please do not feel like your child is regressing; it is the complete opposite. They are progressing and individual instruction can only help that process move forward. There are many parents of typically developing children who would love for their child to be given the opportunity for free tutoring during the regular school day. If you will approach this extra help with the mindset that it is in the best interest of your child and this added benefit will ensure that they are successful in school there will be a positive outcome. Your child will look to you for guidance and reassurance. If you are being positive about what is happening with her education then so will she.

Being a part of your child's educational team should be empowering, knowing that your voice is truly being heard and that her needs are and will continue to be met during her educational career. What it should not be is a nerve racking experience that leaves you emotionally drained. That is why being a team player is so important. Get to know the faculty, communicate often with the teachers, attend conferences and open houses, volunteer in your child's classroom and let the school know that you are intimately involved in your child's life. Your teachers and administrators will appreciate you and your dedication to enhancing the education of not only your child, but for all the children in their school.

A Few of My Favorite Things

"Sometimes you will never know the value of a moment until it is a memory"
— Dr. Seuss

My favorite type of teacher workshop is what we call "make and take" workshops. They are exactly that. Teachers get to spend time creating, constructing, or developing things that they can take with them and immediately use in their classrooms the very next day. I thought I would share some of my favorite recipes, activities and sensory projects. I must warn you, some of them are very messy! That's what makes them FUN! Everything is non-toxic and can be cleaned up with warm water and a towel, or you can do what I do. I have several shower curtains and vinyl table cloths that I put underneath where we are playing, and then I can either pick them up, hose them off or if they are really messy just throw them away. Many of these things are for my sand/water table, but can easily be adapted for home use. I have reduced the recipe portions to be more appropriate for you. Just purchase some medium sized plastic basins with lids, boot storage containers work great, that way you can reuse them for different activities. Ok, let's get started.

Homemade Play Dough

1 Cup flour
½ Cup salt
3 Teaspoons cream of tartar
2 Tablespoons oil
1 Cup Water

Mix the dry ingredients, add water and oil. Cook over low heat, stirring continuously. Cook until mixture thickens and forms a large ball when stirring. Remove from heat and knead on a cutting board until smooth. If you want to add food coloring or scent (use spices such as cinnamon, peppermint, or cherry) put them in the liquid before you add them to dry ingredients. If you forget to put them in, it is no big deal, I have added them during the cooking process and it still works, just takes a little more stirring. This play dough will last for a couple of weeks if you and your child remember to seal the container that you are storing it in after you are finished playing with it.

I like this play dough so much better than the store bought kind for several reasons: it doesn't have that smell that store bought does, some people like it; I do not. It is much more pliable and small children can manipulate it easier, and it comes up out of the carpet super easy! Just let it dry, scrape with a butter knife

and vacuum.   There are many different recipes for play dough and I have tried several of
them. In my opinion this one is the absolute
best! Thank you Ms. Jane ☺

Colored rice
1 box or bag of white rice
½ capful of rubbing alcohol
Food coloring
Place the rice in the container you plan to
play with it in.   Drizzle the rubbing alcohol
over the rice and then drip the desired color of
food coloring on the rice as well. Stir with a
large spoon not your hands; the food coloring
will stain them. If you keep this one sealed you
can keep it indefinitely. One word of advice, do
not add too much alcohol, it will take forever
to evaporate and your whole house will smell
like a hospital. Believe me on this one! I'll just
leave it at that.

Homemade Puff Paint
Shaving cream (not the gel kind)
1 Tablespoon of Borax
Liquid tempura paint
I have also added white tooth paste
to this recipe so that it gives it a
nice minty smell.
Stir all ingredients gently then
brush onto picture
I use this when we paint snowmen
and polar bears

Homemade Finger Paint

Tbs. sugar
½   tsp salt
½   cup corn starch
cups water

Combine all the ingredients in a small sauce pan. Warm until it thickens, you will think it is not going to and then all of the sudden it will look like glycerin, that's what you want. Let it cool and scoop into small containers with lids. Add food coloring at this time that way you can have several different colors from one batch. This stuff is Awesome!

Bubble Clay

Dish soap
Corn starch

There is no measuring to this one, just add dish soap to corn starch and stir until you get the consistency that want. The great thing about this one is when you're done just rinse your hands in the sink and the soap from the clay will wash your hands. Clean-up is a snap!

Goo

1 box corn starch
½ Cup Tap water
Food coloring

Put food coloring into the water and then add all ingredients together in the container. Use your hands to blend completely. Add more water if needed. The consistency should form a solid when you squeeze it and immediately turn back into a liquid when you open your hand. This is one of my favorite sensory activities. I usually make it orange at Halloween and then brown in the spring to simulate mud. This one is messy, but again, if it gets on your carpet just let it dry, scrape with a butter knife and vacuum it up.

Sensory Bucket Ideas

Not everything needs to be made. There are several things that I put in my sensory table that can just be bought and "dumped" in. I change mine with the themes that I do in my classroom which changes every two weeks. Kids just love to put their hands into the different textures. Add some shovels, cups, tongs, funnels, etc. this is always my students favorite center. They cannot wait to see what will be in the sensory table when we change themes. Here is a sampling:

Feed corn (go to the feed and seed store in your area)

Sand: regular sandbox or colored sand (green, purple, red)

Dirt: drive vehicles in it or plant a pretend garden

Large cotton balls and fake snow

Dried beans of all kinds

Cooked and cooled spaghetti (put some veg. oil on it so it will separate)

Corn meal

And don't forget good ole water, add some kids shampoo or bubble bath to give it bubbles and a pleasing smell

Industrial Strength Bubbles
6 Cups water

Cup corn syrup

Cups regular strength Joy dish soap

These are the bubbles that you can use a kiddie pool, a large wand or hula hoop and make a gigantic bubble around the child! Awesome!!!!! (you can also just use them as regular bubbles)

For the Reluctant Eater

If your child is one of those kiddos that doesn't want to try new foods try putting some pudding, applesauce, jello, mashed potatoes, gravy, or ketchup (everything's better with ketchup) on a tray with some food you want them to experience. You can mix them together or just close enough so they will touch when your child scoops up the food they like. Yes, this is messy, but it will get your child to eat a variety of foods. PLEASE remember, messes can be cleaned up. It is not the end of the world if your floor gets food on it. If it really bothers you put down the shower curtain or vinyl tablecloth that I mentioned earlier.

FINALLY...

As you have probably realized, I am all about the process of allowing children to explore their world in a very hands on approach. This is how they learn. I can't tell you how many times I have heard these words "She puts everything in her mouth." or "He smears everything all over him." That is because that is how children instinctively experience new things, by seeing, feeling, smelling, hearing, and yes tasting it. Don't be discouraged, use this to your advantage and help your child get their sensory desires met by introducing some of the activities listed in this chapter. Sometimes we as adults need to let our own guard down and just enjoy the moment with our children. That is my wish for you, if you will try some of these recipes and activities. Yes, there will be a mess, and yes, it will have to be cleaned up. There will also be some special moments that will turn into special memories that will long out live the mess. Enjoy!!!

Some Helpful Resources

"We can't help everyone, but everyone can help someone."
— Ronald Reagan

The intent of this chapter is to help parents/ guardians navigate through the maze of information and resources available to them regarding their child living with developmental delay. It is my hope that the resources I have chosen to include will be helpful and informative. I realize that several of these resources are state specific to Oklahoma; however I have tried to add a side note when appropriate as to how to obtain the same information from the state that you are living in.

Many of the websites are an umbrella site and more specific programs are imbedded within them. For example the website ODDC is a parent organization that has several wonderful programs such as Oklahoma Partners in Policymaking , Oklahoma Youth Leadership Forum, Sibshop, and Disabilities Information Gateway just to name a few.

I encourage you to spend some time browsing through the different sites that you feel might be beneficial to you and your family's specific needs. Those needs will change over the years so keep this guide handy so that you can refer back to it when the need arises.

Agency	Explanation of services provided by each resource	***=very informative **=informative *=least informative
Interagency Coordinating Council (ICC) In OK this is the SoonerStart Program (search interagency coordinating council for your state)	Early intervention program designed to meet the needs of infants and toddlers with disabilities and developmental delays	***
Developmental Disabilities Services Division (DDSD) http://www.okdhs.org/programsandservices/dd/ other states: www.hhs.gov	Provides services to persons ages 3 and older who have a primary diagnosis of intellectual disability	***
Supplemental Security Income (SSI) ssa.gov/pgm/ssi.htm	Benefits (monthly checks) for children younger than 18 based on their disability and family income	***
Oklahoma Department of Human Services (OKDHS) http://www.okdhs.org/	Offers services and programs for persons with disabilities	***
Oklahoma Developmental Disability Council (ODDC) Partners in Policymaking and Youth Leadership Forum http://www.okddc.state.ok.us/	Promotes services and programs that enable persons with developmental disabilities to be independent and productive through integration and inclusion into the community	**

Oklahoma ABLE Tech http://okabletech.okstate.edu	Making assistive technology devices and services more available and accessible to individuals with disabilities and their families	**
Oklahoma Family Network www.oklahomafamilynetwork.org	A parent-to-parent group advocating for family centered care for those who are raising children with special health care needs	**
Oklahoma Library for the Blind and Physically Handicapped library@drs.state.ok.us	Provides free services to Oklahomans who are blind or visually impaired and those with learning disabilities or physical limitations that make it difficult to use standard print	**
Oklahoma School for the Blind www.osb.k12.ok.us/index.html/	The school's purpose is to meet the educational needs of blind and visually impaired students who are residents of the state by providing a program to help students reach their maximum potential.	**
Smart Start Search SmartStart for your state	Advances community efforts that assure quality experiences and opportunities for children from birth to 6 through education, resource sharing, and communication	**

Oklahoma School for the Deaf www.osd.k12.ok.us	Is a residential or daily drop off school where sports, daily living, class instruction, and dorm life is geared to his/her special communication needs.	**
Vocational Rehabilitation(VR)/Department of Rehabilitation Services(DRS) www.okrehab.org or www.okdrs.gov	Provides services for individuals who have a physical or mental disability that keeps you from working, the services will help you prepare, find, and keep a job	**
Oklahoma Areawide Services Information System (OASIS) www.oasis.ouhsc.edu	Provides free statewide information, referral, and one-on-one assistance in locating available services in Oklahoma	**
Yellow Pages for Kids http://www.yellowpagesfor kids.com	for children with disabilities across all 50 states Provides numerous resources	*
National Dissemination Center for Children with Disabilities (NICHCY) www.nichcy.org	serves as a central source of information: click the national map in the lower right hand corner	*
Zarrow Center for Learning Enrichment http://education.ou.edu/zarrow	Facilitates successful secondary and postsecondary educational, vocational and personal outcomes for students and adults with disabilities.	**

Resource	Description	Rating
National Early Childhood Transition Center(NECTC) http://www.hdi.uky.edu/NECTC/practicesearch.aspx	Examine factors that promote successful transitions between infant/toddler programs, preschool programs, and public school programs for young children with disabilities and their families	**
National Downs Syndrome Society www.ndss.org	Raises awareness of Downs Syndrome in the community, provides resources for support and education to families of children living with Downs Syndrome	**
People First http://www.disabilityisnatural.com/	People First Language (PFL) represents more respectful, accurate ways of communicating. People with disabilities are not their diagnoses or disabilities; they are people, first.	**
TEFRA: Tax Equity and Fiscal Responsibility Act of 1982 (allows for children to be cared for in their home) For OK residents: www.okhca.org/TEFRA Other states: go to your stated Healthcare Authority website	Gives states the option to make Medicaid benefits available to children with physical or mental disabilities who would not ordinarily be eligible for SSI benefits	*

Appendix

Figure 1. Sound reduction headphones block out extraneous noise.

Figure 2. Homemade weighted vest; they are less expensive and more versatile because you can increase or decrease the weight as needed.

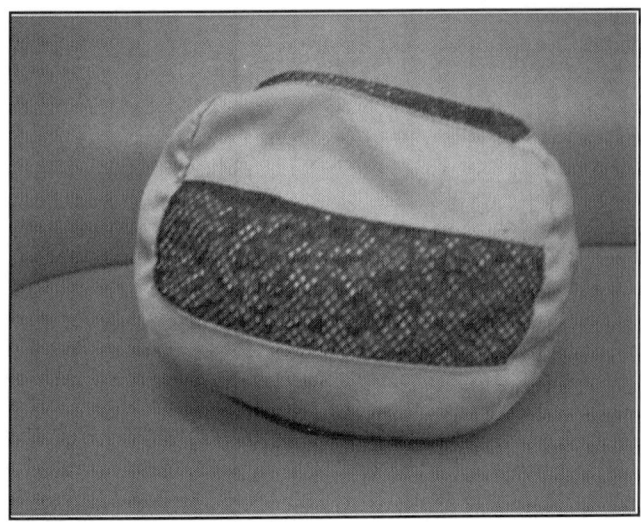

Figure 3. Squishy balls are easier to catch and throw.

Figure 4. Texture panels – children love
to feel the contrasts of textures.

Figure 5. Sensory ball weighted, auditory, and visual. This is great for hearing- and visually-impaired children.

Figure 6. Picture schedules help
your child see what their day will
look like (see page 22).

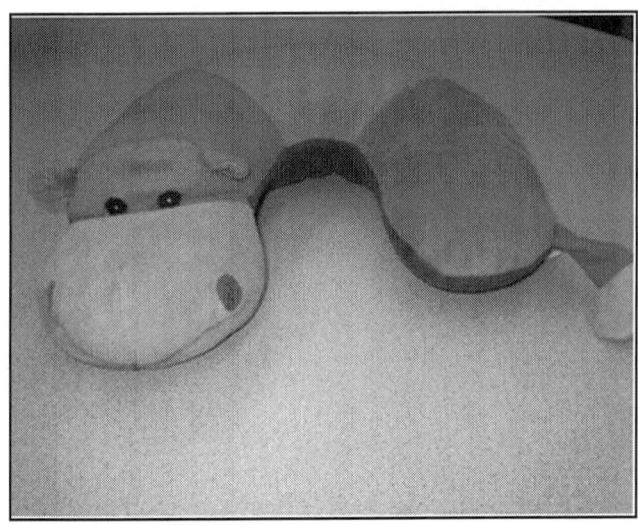

Figure 7. A weighted shoulder snuggler gives your child a personalized "hug."

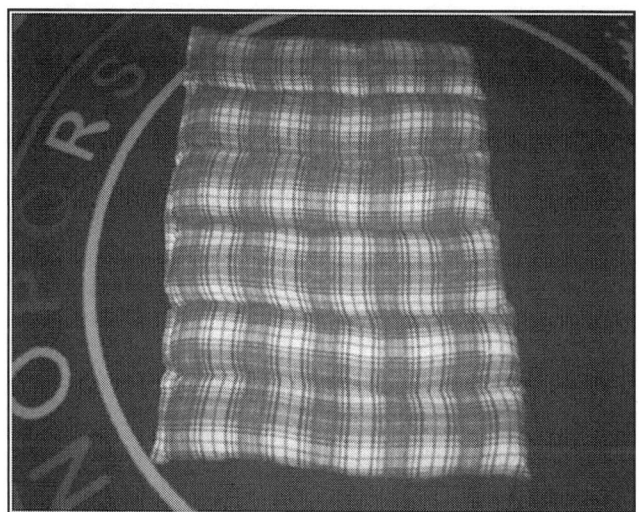

Figure 8. A homemade weighted blanket helps some children feel safe when it's time for bed.

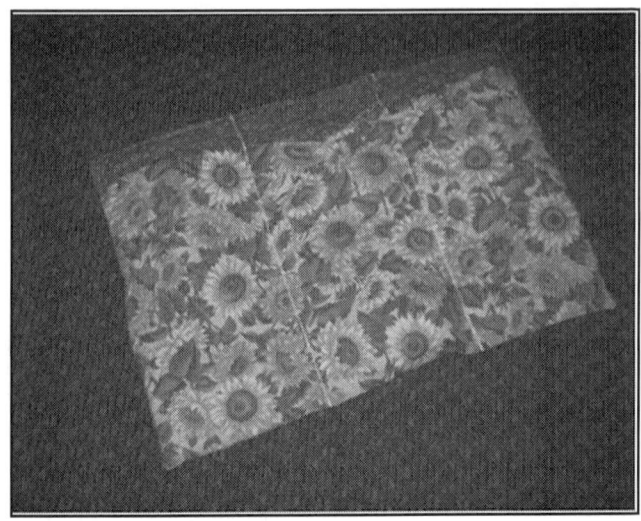

Figure 9. Another homemade weighted blanket.

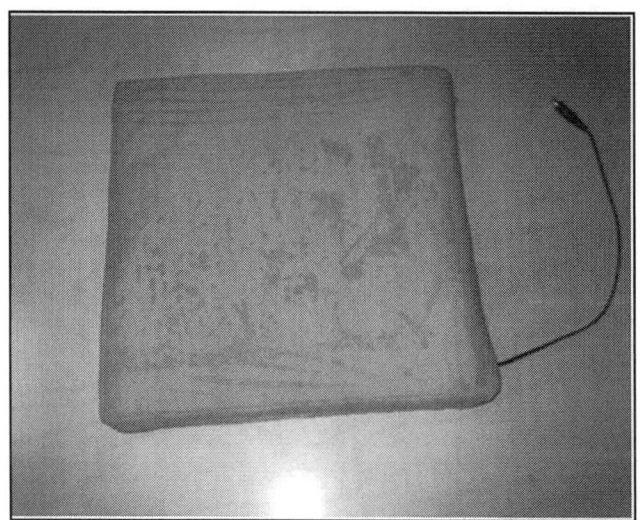

Figure 10. A vibration pad – for some children vibration helps to calm them down.

About the Author

Robin Atkinson has been teaching Special Education for 25 years. She received her Bachelor of Science Degree in Special Education from the University of Oklahoma and her Master's degree in Learning and Leadership with an emphasis in Special Education from Oklahoma State University.

Robin has taught special education in different regions across the country and in a variety of settings: the traditional public school, the self-contained classroom, the inclusive classroom, and the residential facility classroom. She has also worked in the extended school program setting as well as the homebound instruction setting.

Robin began her teaching in 1985 where she taught in Norman, Oklahoma, in the late 1990's she moved to North Carolina where she taught as well, but as a native Oklahoman, her roots kept calling her home. In 2001 she moved to Stillwater, Oklahoma where she lives today with her teenage son and their dog Rose. She currently serves the Stillwater public school system as the District Special Education Teacher for the 3 year old Developmentally Delayed Program.

66793787R00049

Made in the USA
Lexington, KY
24 August 2017